Rule of

Thumb

A Guide to Developing Mission, Vision, and Value Statements

Sonia Keffer

Text Copyright © 2014, 2023 Sonia Keffer

Published by
ParkerStreetGroup.com

Printed in the United States of America

ISBN: 979-8-9876591-0-6 (p)
ISBN: 979-8-9876591-1-3 (e)

Second Edition

Find out more information @ SoniaKeffer.com

Dedication

To everyone with an idea. May you believe in your dreams and take every step possible to create the reality you wish to live in.

Many, many thanks to Michael Mitilier, Scott Hevelone, Julie Jahde Pospishil, and my family for their encouragement of my writing process.

Contents

Chapter 1 **What will this book do for me?**

Welcome to *A Guide to Developing Mission, Vision, and Value Statements.* This guide presents a clear, easy to follow, and comprehensive process for developing and using your organization's mission, vision, and value statements which I have gleaned from nearly fifteen years of helping companies navigate successful implementation of these valuable tools.

My career began as a facilitator of Job Search workshops, helping people receiving government assistance move toward a more self-sufficient lifestyle. At this job with Curtis and Associates, Inc., I first became acquainted with the power of a company's mission statement. I worked at other companies with mission statements, but rarely heard or saw them beyond day one orientation. At Curtis and Associates, Inc., not only did I regularly see the mission statement, but understood it as a mandate to be lived each day in each of our offices across the United States. This company held contracts across the country to deliver job readiness, job search, and case management services for state and local governments during the welfare reform push of the 1990s.

As a for profit company in a very public business, we were an anomaly; we had to continually be able to talk about who we were and what we were about.

We had to do this in order to help government employees understand why we were in their "territory." Our mission statement and guiding principles (value statements) were the best way to relay our message. The company has since been sold, but I still have my laminated card with the mission statement and guiding principles. They are as follows:

"Curtis & Associates, Inc. will have an international impact on reducing poverty, unemployment, and dependence on social welfare programs. Through its existence, millions of people will have higher self-esteem, higher hopes for the future and jobs that will lift them from the welfare rolls. Governments will save millions of dollars through the efforts of the company.

Our Goal is to motivate people to value and to succeed in securing self-sufficiency. We will do all we can to support and sustain each other as we work together to accomplish this goal."

Teams believe in:
1. Quality
2. Self-sufficiency
3. Customer is #1
4. Fiscal Responsibility
5. Integrity
6. Professionalism
7. Consistency
8. Growth

It is not new for a company to have a mission statement. However, in the late 1980s-early 2000s, it was certainly cutting-edge to make sure each team member had copies of the statements. It was even more cutting edge to begin each and every team meeting by having everyone stand and recite the statement from memory. On more than one occasion I thought I had joined a cult, but the statement was important. It connected each team member with another and kept our primary goals in focus.

This book is about exactly how company mission, vision, and value statements are more than words.

What will I find in this book?

This book provides a background and a practical guide for you, the new or established micro or small business owner, to begin formulating your big idea and sharing it with others in your family, industry, community, and the world.

This book will help you understand:
- What are mission, vision, and value statements.
- Why your company needs these statements.
- What they can do for a for-profit or a nonprofit organization.
- How to develop mission, vision, and value statements.

7

- The importance of sharing the statements once they are developed.
- Who needs to know the mission, vision, and value statements.
- How these statements can guide decision making.
- How mission, vision, and value statements can guide human resource decisions.
- How to utilize mission, vision, and value statements in marketing and public relations.
- How to use mission, vision, and value statements in strategic planning.

It is one thing to have a developed set of mission, vision, and value statements, and it is another thing to live your statements in every relationship and every interaction.

Chapter 2: What are Mission, Vision, and Value Statements?

Before you can begin to identify a company mission, vision, or value statement, you must understand what each represents and why they are important enough to develop. In his book, *Vision: How Leaders Develop It, Share It, and Sustain It,* each of these statements make up what author Joseph V. Quigley calls an organization's "Vision." Quigley asserts organizations must have a clearly thought-out plan for their existence and future. A Vision is what leaders develop as a road map for helping the organization reach its goals and make progress to the future. Vision can then be a good overarching title for the three individual statements, with each statement making up a part of the road map for a company's success. Throughout this book, you will notice that when I speak of the overarching Vision it will be capitalized for emphasis and differentiation from the vision statement.

As I have assisted companies in developing their primary Vision statement, I typically find most people have heard of a mission statement, but value and vision statements are foreign concepts. This is partly due to the mission statement being more public, while the value and vision statements are more internal, informing employees how to live out the mission.

9

Value and vision statements tend to be for internal eyes only. We use them with our teams, board members, and shareholders who understand how we operate and how we wish to operate in the future, but it may be information we may not be ready to open up to public scrutiny. Many companies, however, do publish their entire Vision statement. These companies take a position of transparency with their customers and community. As you work your way through this book and the development of your Vision, how much you share will be a question to contemplate. Let's begin by further defining the mission, vision, and value statements.

What is the Mission Statement?

The mission statement is a sentence or two to a short paragraph which explains "why we exist." According to, *Executive Director's Guide: The Guide for Successful Nonprofit Management,* "the mission statement describes the overarching purpose of the organization." The authors further explain how putting a focus on mission "gives clarity to staff and other key stakeholders about why they are there." For a relatively short statement, the expectation of the mission statement is to give everyone (inside and outside of the organization) the reason the business exists.

In its simplest form, the mission statement answers three questions:

1. Why do we exist?
2. Who do we serve?
3. What do we produce?

Here is an example of a mission statement from Lowe's home improvement stores:

"Together, deliver the right home improvement products, with the best service and value, across every channel and community we serve."

This simple statement tells us all we need to know about why Lowe's is in business, "together" tells us their customer is a major part of the business model. "...best service and value" tells us they work to provide stellar customer service and product prices that will beat their competition to serve their customers.

What is the Vision Statement?

Where the mission explains why the organization exists and the work it does every day, the vision statement sets a long-term goal for the organization. The vision statement, according to *Executive Director's Guide: The Guide for Successful Nonprofit Management* is "the picture of the future that the organization seeks to create." "Holding a vision helps us decide which strategies to implement in actualizing our mission."

The vision statement is a very short phrase or sentence that sets an exciting tone for planning the future of the organization. It is the organization's shared hopes, dreams, and image of the future. The vision statement answers:

What do we want to become in the future?

Here are some examples of vision statements from Nike:

- 1960s: "Crush Adidas"
- 2014: "To be the number one athletic company in the world."
- Current: "Do everything possible to expand human potential."

Jose Luis Romeo, on his website, www.Skills2Lead.com, defines the vision statements beautifully as, "… something you want to become, to achieve, it is a seductive image of an ideal future." Nike's statements do just that. They don't give us specific deadlines, but they create a spirit of action which can be translated into specific, measurable goals by teams, departments, and individuals within the organization. The vision statement inspires growth and gives direction to achieve our mission every day.

The basis of any organization is its values. For a company to reach its vision the values must be uncovered and defined. Let's venture on to define the value statement.

What is the Value Statement?

The best way to describe the value statement is by using the metaphor of a building's foundation. The foundation of a home is usually made of some sturdy material like concrete blocks, no matter what homeowners might do to the rest of their structure, paint, redecorate, remove a wall, add a room or an entire floor, rarely does one replace the foundation of the home. Values are like a home's basement or foundation. They are what exist in the company. The value statement is actually a series of words with definitions representing the organization's core beliefs. You may also hear core values referred to as "guiding principles." They represent how the organization operates—how team members act with one another. Simply stated, again by the authors of *Executive Directors Guide: The Guide for Successful Nonprofit Management*, "Values are our beliefs in action—they guide our behavior as we take action to realize our vision and purpose (mission)."

The value statement answers the question:

What do we stand for?

Look at this example of a value statement from IKEA,

Lead by Example: We see leadership as an action, not a position. We look for people's values before competence and experience. People who 'walk the talk' and lead by example. It is about being our best self and bringing out the best in each other.

Togetherness: Togetherness is at the heart of the IKEA culture. We are strong when we trust each other, pull in the same direction, and have fun together.

Caring for People and Planet: We want to be a force for positive change. We have the possibility to make a significant and lasting impact - today and for the generations to come.

Cost-Consciousness: As many people as possible should be able to afford a beautiful and functional home. We constantly challenge ourselves and others to make more from less without compromising on quality.

Simplicity: A simple, straightforward, and down-to-earth way of being is part of our Småland heritage. It is about being ourselves and staying close to reality. We are informal, pragmatic and see bureaucracy as our biggest enemy.

Renew and Improve: We are constantly looking for new and better ways forward. Whatever we are doing today, we can do better tomorrow. Finding solutions to almost impossible challenges is part of our success and a source of inspiration to move on to the next challenge.

Different with a Meaning: IKEA is not like other companies, and we don't want to be. We like to question existing solutions, think in unconventional ways, experiment, and dare to make mistakes - always for a good reason.

Give and Take Responsibly: We believe in empowering people. Giving and taking responsibility are ways to grow and develop as individuals. Trusting each other, being positive and forward-looking inspires everyone to contribute to development.

Typically, organizations will highlight 4 to 8 values that they want to set as the standard of behavior. Each of the value words that IKEA uses above could have several definitions; they defined each the way they want their team members to understand them in their workplace. Remember, your organization determines what it values and the definition of each value. Those definitions are what you want to highlight for your team and stakeholders.

A reminder from Quigley, "defining corporate values or making them explicit does clearly show the corporation's intention to foster those values." My advice is to define the values you believe to be the core of the company, and then, live those values in every interaction with everyone.

Rule of Thumb:
The overall "Vision" statement mentioned earlier is then a series of three statements comprised of the mission statement, which answers, "Why do we exist?" the vision statement, which answers, "What do we want to become in the future?", and the value statement, which answers, "What do we stand for?" Each of these statements creates a baseline of sorts for organizational and business thinking, behavior, and planning.

In the next chapter, we will explore why mission, vision and value statements are important for your organization.

Chapter 3: Why does the Organization need Mission, Vision, and Value Statements?

It may seem obvious to you that there is a need for mission, vision, and value statements. With the abundance of Vision statements that are in the public eye, it may just seem natural that you will have these statements for your organization. Yet, it's still important to ask why. Each organization will have to explore exactly what they want to get out of their Vision and what, exactly, they will use it for. We will explore some ideas on this topic in a later chapter.

In the previous chapter, we looked at what the mission, vision, and value statements are, what they are comprised of, and what they answer for the organization. Understanding what they are can help us understand why they are important. Each statement does something different for the organization. Each represents an aspect of purpose about why the organization was created and why it is in business.

It is true many organizations have been successful without a Vision statement. Typically, these organizations have been started by a single high achieving individual who dictates all internal and external movement of the organization. Then, when the owner sells the business or retires, the organization peters out over time or crumbles quickly because the person with the vision is no longer at the helm.

The primary benefit of having a Vision statement is that it allows the organization to function as a unified entity with many intelligent people sharing the same central reason for doing what they do. This Vision allows those caring individuals to work together to set meaningful and achievable goals for the organization's present work and future aspirations. In addition, it allows them to make decisions about everyday behavior. What is behavior in a business? It is both how we handle any situation that comes up, and, how we expect team members and leaders to interact with one another and with our customers.

Rule of Thumb:
Having a company Vision brings every member of the team to the table with the same information about how the company founders want it to be run.

The second thing a Vision statement does for your organization is build trust in the workplace. In his book *The Speed of Trust: The one thing that changes everything*, Stephen M. R. Covey (Stephen Covey's son and the former CEO of the Covey Leadership Center) talks about a simple equation for trust.

He says, "Trust is the function of two things: character and competence. Character includes your integrity, your motive, and your intent with people. Competence includes your capabilities, your skills, your results, and your track record. Both are vital." The way I describe it is, Trust = Integrity + Competence. Before the leadership team buys into what the CEO or Board of Directors is saying, there must be trust. Leaders must believe the CEO and/ or Board are acting with the deepest sense of integrity when it comes to business matters; just as importantly, they must believe that the CEO or Board are competent in leading the organization forward.

When the Vision is communicated clearly and applied consistently, trust is achieved, creating a culture where people are committed to helping each other live out the Vision.

Rule of Thumb:
Trust = Integrity + Competence
Trust is grown by living the
company Vision statement.

This certainly funnels down to all layers of the organization. Once the leadership team has the Vision, they need to share it and prove they are trustworthy and competent with their team members.

Trust enables things to get done in teams, workgroups, communities, and life, by creating an environment where people don't question one another's motives and priorities. When the core of trust is built on your Vision, then it can be seen and measured by everyone in the organization. You know if team members are living their values by the way they work with peers and customers. You know the organization is living its mission everyday by the work that is produced. You know the company is working toward its vision if the annual strategic plan has the vision as its ultimate goal.

The third effect: it becomes a compass for the organization. A compass is the instrument of direction which is clear and obvious to everyone in the organization. In his book, *Principle Centered Leadership,* Stephen R. Covey describes how individual leaders and organizations must work diligently to make their Vision more than just words and base them on strong, natural laws we understand and relate to. He refers to these as natural principles. In terms of business principles, or values, he says, "I find a universal belief in fairness, kindness, dignity, charity, integrity, honesty, quality, service, and patience." He continues, "Consider the absurdity of trying to live a life or run a business based on the opposites."

Do you recognize some of these values in your company already? You may choose to use all of Covey's natural principles as your company's values, or you may choose our own, just bear in mind the compass effect that they will have on your company.

Rule of Thumb:
Let your organization's Vision be a compass to guide the company in everyday behavior, as well as long term planning and growth.

As this book goes into more depth about developing value statements you will see these values come up repeatedly. According to Covey, "These principles surface time and again, and the degree to which people in a society recognize and live in harmony with them moves them toward either survival and stability or disintegration and destruction."

By creating your organization's Vision, you are creating the ability for the organization to succeed in meeting its goals. By borrowing Covey's compass, we are giving ourselves and our organization the ability to succeed in any business climate, which can change at any moment, usually, when we least expect it.

"The compass orients people to the coordinates and indicates a course of direction even in forests, deserts, seas, and open unsettled terrain" says Covey. The organizational Vision will help everyone involved in the business know which direction to go, literally and metaphorically.

Our Vision provides the foundation for the set of rules with which our organization will operate. In a sense, the Vision runs the company, providing the direction for all our activities. By setting up a powerful, value-based Vision for your organization, you are sharing a set of guiding rules everyone can see, learn, understand, and follow. In doing so, you are building the basis of a long-lasting organization that can grow and change as the environment demands.

Practically speaking, different organizations will have different needs for having a Vision statement. The ideas we've discussed so far are three big ones that will affect all organizations, regardless of their size. The needs of for-profit organizations and not-for profit organizations may have slight variations which are worth exploring, but generally those differences come down to funding sources and justifying budgets. (See *Rule of Thumb: Guide to Business Basics* for more information on taxation status and organizational structure options you may want to explore.)

Anyone can create a Vision for their organization; the real challenge is to understand why you need the statement and what it will do for your company, whether you realize its potential power or not. If you are like many business owners or managers, you want your initial business idea to become a great addition to your community and to bring you career stability. To achieve this, you must write your mission, vision, and value statements with the intent of having them dictate the direction of the organization as an independent entity beyond you. You must share the Vision in order to build organizational trust so the business can grow, and finally, if you want your company to be successful well beyond you and your initial idea, then you must write your mission, vision, and value statements, as a compass which will allow anyone involved with the organization to maneuver the challenging roads that the business may encounter.

Chapter 4: Developing Mission, Vision, and Value Statements

Hopefully you are excited about what the mission, vision, and value statements stand for and understand why them having can positively impact the success of your organization. You may be inspired by a few of the sample statements you've read so far in this book or one you've seen at another business. However, one question may still remain unanswered: how do I develop one for my organization? This is understandably a difficult question to answer because there are many approaches to developing them.

There are many examples of mission, vision, and value statements online. One way to develop your statements is to sift through the results of a search and piece together a Vision that sounds like your company or the company you aspire to become. I think looking at all your available resources is a wise move, and yet I would discourage anyone from just "borrowing" a set of mission, vision, and value statements from other organizations. These statements ultimately represent you and your company, and you don't want to be just a copycat version of someone else's Vision.

Check out some examples of mission, vision, and value statements before you begin developing your own. Make notes and jot down words or phrases that resonate with you.

Most people find words that inspire feeling and emotion are often the most powerful when it comes to mission, vision, and value statements. You need to also look closely at design. How do different companies structure their statements? Do they use a paragraph format or a bullet-pointed list to share their Vision with the rest of the world? Which one do you find is more pleasant to look at and easy to understand? Consider sharing the statement with others: customers, suppliers, partners, and trusted advisors in your professional network. If you were making a presentation about your organization's Vision, which style would help you talk about it most easily? Many of us are visual learners, so having a finished product that also makes a visual statement will be easier for others to understand and put into daily action.

Rule of Thumb:
Before developing your business's Vision statement, take time to check out other organization's statements. Get a feel for structure and wording that appeals to you.

Developing your organization's statements

If you are a sole proprietor organization, you may write your statements by yourself. I would suggest you share your creation with other significant people in your life, such as, family, friends, a mentor, and trusted business associates. Each person's opinion will give you insight into what message your statements send about your company. There is no timeline for writing your Vision, yet you will want to create one early enough that it begins to drive your organization in the direction you desire.

As you will learn in a future chapter, your Vision will make leading your organization clearer. Having a Vision statement is often a requirement if you are applying for non-profit status or grant funding, so it is important to put time into developing it early in the game. Take some time, listen to important people's ideas, and decide on your final statements. The beauty of this process is you can modify statements when one has become outdated, or a goal has been met. I would caution against doing it very often, but mission, vision, and value statements can certainly be evaluated at yearly strategic planning meetings.

If you are part of a partnership or small business, then it is important to include those most integral to the company's success in the development of the Vision.

Partners would want to use the same process outlined above. If you have a small team already in place, say 5-10 members, you could enlist everyone's help or only those three or four who represent specific and important aspects of the business.

It is always best to try to have major areas of operation represented on the development team, just as it is important to enlist the help of those with varied opinions to help with the process.

> **Rule of Thumb:**
> Developing your company's Vision statement can be done by yourself, individually, with a group of your coworkers, or with the help of a third-party consultant. Hiring a consultant can free you and the development team from the work of preparing and planning and allow you to truly participate in the process of development.

The last thing you want is to create a groupthink atmosphere where debate and discussion don't happen at all. The best company Vision is developed through a process of creation, deletion, and re-creation, always working toward the most succinct statement that describes your organization.

You may find that the process of creating your statements brings out strong opinions from team members, but when managed well this can help clarify the direction you want to go in together.

Of course, developing your Vision is work you can do by yourself (including those who are most integral to your business); however, there is another way that can prove insightful and helpful no matter the size or scope of your business. Hiring a consultant to help facilitate the development process can allow you and the designated key players to participate in the process without having to organize and run meetings, in addition to being a part of the Vision statement development team.

A consultant can plan the development process to suit your organization's needs. He or she can help you decide who would be best to have on the development team. A consultant can also aid in deciding how many meetings would be best to develop the Vision, bringing resources to the table you may not readily have access to. Also, he or she can act as a sounding board for the ideas that the development team brainstorms. Most importantly, the consultant is a neutral third party in the process, which allows him or her to ask questions of the development team they may not otherwise ask each other.

A consultant may have ideas to share that your development team has not thought of; although the role of the consultant is to ultimately facilitate the development process for your group, as opposed to creating the statement for you.

Consider hiring a consultant if you find it is hard to get started, hard to get the group together because of other work duties, or if you've started the process, but keep stopping and re-starting without accomplishing your goal of having an organizational Vision completed for your business.

The next several sections of this book will give you some basic guidelines for developing your organization's Vision. These can be done individually, in small groups, with or without the help of a third-party consultant.

Chapter 5: Developing the Organization's Value Statement

As this book has talked about mission, vision, and value statements, it may seem this is the order in which you should develop them. Yet I believe it is best to develop your statements in a slightly different order. When I work with organizations, I ask them to start by developing their value statement, then move to vision statement, and finally end with the mission statement. Why not just jump into the mission statement? Well, I believe before you can fully answer what you do, you must answer what you stand for. Think of the value statement as the foundation upon which your organization stands. If you recall the metaphor from chapter 2, while you might remodel your home, rarely do you tear out the basement and rebuild it. The foundation, or what you stand for, is a solid structure that will rarely change. If you know what your organization stands for, building the vision and the mission statements will flow more easily.

Next, I ask companies to think into the future and create their vision statement, or where they want to be in the future. Knowing what we base our organization on (values) as well as where we aspire to be in the future (vision) will help us understand what we need to work on every day, when it comes time to write the mission statement, which is the last statement that I have organizations develop. By waiting until the value and vision statements have been created, the mission statement writes itself. What we do is more easily stated when we know what we stand for and where we want to go.

How to Develop the Value Statement

As you will remember from an earlier chapter, the value statement answers the basic question, "What do we stand for?" When given a little more thought, you will realize that this question is anything but simple. There are many reasons for having a written value statement, including:

- People demonstrate and model the values in action in their personal work behaviors, decision making, contribution, and interpersonal interaction.
- Organizational values help people establish priorities in their daily work lives.

- Values guide every decision that is made once the organization has cooperatively created the values and the value statements.
- Rewards and recognition within the organization are structured to recognize those people whose work embodies the values the organization embraces.
- Organizational goals are grounded in the identified values.
- Adaptation of the values and the behaviors that result are recognized in regular performance feedback.
- People hire and promote individuals whose outlook and actions are congruent with the values.

We all have personal values in the form of our ethics and morals. Taking the step of developing a value statement for your business is equal to standing up in front of your organization, board members, shareholders, customers, the entire community, and saying to them, this is what our company believes is most important. This is how we operate our business and treat our employees and customers. When you do business with us, this is what you'll get. Please hold us to these core values.

To develop your value statement, it is good to look at some examples. Look below. As you read through them, note words or phrases that sound like your company. This could mean what you currently stand for or what you would like to be known for.

Whole Foods Market

- We Sell the Highest Quality Natural & Organic Foods
- We Satisfy and Delight our Customers
- We Promote Team Member Growth and Happiness
- We Practice Win-win Partnerships with our Suppliers
- We Create Profits and Prosperity
- We Care about Our Communities adn Our Environment

Zappos Family

As we grow as a company, it has become more and more important to explicitly define the core values from which we develop our culture, our brand, and our business strategies. These are the ten core values that we live by:

- Deliver WOW Through Service
- Embrace and Drive Change
- Create Fun and A Little Weirdness
- Be Adventurous, Creative, and Open-Minded

- Pursue Growth and Learning
- Build Open and Honest Relationships With Communication
- Build a Positive Team and Family Spirit
- Do More with Less
- Be Passionate and Determined
- Be Humble

Fashion Cleaners

- **Serve the Customer:** We anticipate and meet the needs of all of our customers in a timely manner, bringing enthusiasm and knowledge to each customer served.
- **Quality:** We take pride in the superior value of the services we deliver to our customers through our experienced staff.
- **Communication:** We believe in honest, timely, and informative communication.
- **Training:** We provide training which strengthens internal morale, teamwork, and personal and professional growth.

Professional Veterinary Services, Ltd.

- We focus on a future of growth and change through innovative ideas, planning, and continuous improvement.
- We focus on strong employee, customer, and vendor relationships by approaching every interaction with honesty and integrity.
- We focus on providing superior service to our customers with commitment to quality and value.
- We focus on providing a caring, family-oriented environment which encourages our employees to grow professionally and personally.
- We focus on consistent, honest, and responsible communication that facilitates cooperation and accountability.
  We focus on the responsible use of resources to sustain the financial viability of our company.

Oregon Shakespeare Festival

These are the values we hold at the Oregon Shakespeare Festival. They are at the center of everything we do and describe how we work together. While we recognize the need for balance among them, these values guide us in all our decisions:

- **Excellence**: We believe in constantly seeking to present work of the highest quality, expecting excellence from all company members.

- **Inclusion**: We believe the inclusion of a diversity of people, ideas, and cultures enriches both our insights into the work we present on stage and our relationships with each other.

- **Learning**: We believe in offering company members, audiences, teachers, and students the richest possible learning experiences.

- **Financial Health**: We believe in continuing our long history of financial stability, making wise and efficient use of all the resources entrusted to us.

- **Heritage**: We believe that the festival's history of almost seventy-five years gives us a heritage of thoughtful change and evolution to guide us as we face the future.

Teach for America

- **Pursue Equity:** We work to change practices, structures, and policies to realize educational equity for all children. As we do so, we actively examine our roles in perpetuating inequitable systems.

- **Strengthen Community:** We assume responsibility for our collective strength by developing relationships, building diverse and inclusive coalitions, and challenging one another to be our best. We act with empathy and extend grace to ourselves and others.

- **Achieve Impact:** We pursue ambitious, meaningful outcomes that lead to access and opportunity for all children. We hold ourselves to high standards, make data-informed decisions, and orient to long-term success.

- **Choose Courage:** We act on our beliefs and values, especially when it's hard. We center our efforts on the aspirations of our students and their families.

- **Act With Humility:** We acknowledge the limitations of our perspectives. We seek different points of view and historical context to evolve our thinking and actions.

37

- **Demonstrate Resilience:** We see every challenge as an opportunity to think expansively about solutions. When faced with obstacles, we deepen our resolve, adapt, and persist with optimism.
- **Learn Continuously:** We operate with curiosity and embrace new ideas to innovate and constantly improve. We take informed risks and learn from successes, setbacks, and each other.

As you read through the value statements, I hope you were inspired by many of the words and definitions. When developing the value statement, I tell organizations, it is more about identifying what your values are than trying to write a list of words that sound good or might impress someone else. Since we, as individuals, have our own internal set of values, we automatically bring many of them to our workplaces.

Therefore, we generally don't have to create the company's value statement; we simply have to look at our existing values and articulate them in a meaningful way.

Setting up a Development Team

If you choose to create a development team instead of going it alone, it is time to assemble your team. Spend some time thinking about who you want on your development team. They need to be people you trust and people who understand the business you are starting or currently operating. They need to be people who have more than a passing interest in your business and are committed to your success. They should be people who are not afraid to share their ideas and will provide frank feedback. It is also helpful if you invite people with different areas of expertise to be on the development team. Each will bring varied fields of experience to the table, which will make for a richer experience. They might be mentors, shareholders, and board members. They might be current leaders within your business or current team members. They might even be family members and friends.

The size of the development team will depend on the size of your organization. There is no correct number of development team members, but five to twenty might be right. Typically, more than twelve on the team becomes difficult to manage, unless you have a highly structured process or are using a consultant. Once you have your team in place, you are ready to begin developing your Vision.

> **Rule of Thumb:**
> Embrace diversity of thought, as you put together your development team. Include people from different work groups within the organization so that you avoid groupthink during the development process.

The first step is to uncover your values, and sometimes words don't come as easily as we would like during the development phase. I suggest looking at a list of value words (one has been included in the appendix of this book) as a guide for you and your development team. It is often best to limit the number of value words that you choose to begin the process and then whittle them down further. If you are looking at the list at the back of this book, it may seem a bit overwhelming. Take a few minutes to have each member of the development team read over the list and choose 10-12 words that seem to describe what you, as an organization, stand for.

Once the members have their lists, share them. This can be done simply by setting up a large piece of paper at the front of the room and having someone write the chosen words on the page. Make hash marks for duplicates. At this point, you may be surprised by how in sync the development team is in all the choices.

Next, the team will want to see if some of the value words overlap each other, mean the same thing, or can be combined. It would be a goal at this point to narrow your list of value words to 6-9, with an ultimate goal of having between 4-6 value statements.

There will be quite a bit of discussion about the value words chosen. Some members of the development team will argue the words mean the same thing, while others will emphatically argue they mean something different. You may want to have a dictionary and thesaurus handy for such disputes. Discussion about the value words is very worthwhile, as it ultimately clarifies for the team exactly what you stand for and what message you want to send about your organization. Give this some time. Where our natural inclination would be to end the discussion and to make peace, let the conversation go until a natural resting place emerges.

Once the list of words is chosen, the team will move on to the next step of defining what each word means in terms of your organization. Just like the examples above, your development team (whether in fact a team or just yourself initially) will take time to write out what each of the chosen words means in terms of how your company operates. Again, this process will take time.

I suggest breaking this down into more manageable parts. Here is a simple checklist of how to break your development team into smaller workgroups for maximum effectiveness.

- Break the larger group into smaller groups of 2-5 people. (When dividing your development team members up, keep in mind the need for maximum freedom to brainstorm and minimum interpersonal conflict.)
- Provide tools/resources for brainstorming (note paper, flip chart, markers, and dictionary/ thesaurus)
- Provide historical information on values, value statements, vision statements, and mission statements.
- Give a time frame and clear objectives for the exercise. Remind participants of guidelines for brainstorming. (No bad/wrong ideas, write down everything, generate as many ideas as possible, and evaluate later)

First, have individuals or small groups of 2-5 people define each word or give them one or two words on which to work. Four or five words to define can feel overwhelming. Make sure each team has a copy of the value statement examples from this book and access to resource materials. Give the groups up to thirty minutes to work on this first step.

> **Rule of Thumb:**
> During the development process make sure that you have handy some supplies that allow for creativity, such as, large post-it pages, markers, tape, dictionary, thesaurus, etc. Make the development process as easy to visualize for the group as possible.

When each team has beginning thoughts on the definition of the value words, bring the larger group back together to share their work. This is a time when you will want to have some room to spread out. As most of us are visual learners, I suggest giving each group a large sheet of paper on which to write their definitions. Have each group hang these up on the wall, so everyone can see and study them. Begin with one and work your way through each of the statements. Have the original writers read their statements and explain how they came to feel these definitions describe what the company stands for. At this point the floor is open, and everyone should share their thoughts, questions, concerns, and differing opinions. This is a free and open process of sharing, which means sharing in a spirit of finding the best definitions for the organization.

The final decision must be the best possible definition that the majority of the development team agrees represents the organization in its best light. No one person should be allowed to dominate the conversation or bully the rest of the group into agreeing with their definition. Of course, the original writers will feel some ownership of their definitions, and they, too, will need to be open to the ideas of the group, for the betterment of the whole.

You will want to have an open discussion about each of the values in the statement to come to a consensus on the definition of each. In case that does not happen, we must leave the ultimate bottom line decision, if questions remain, to the CEO or Executive Director of the organization.

It helps to have someone write the changes on the papers on the wall for the group. This could either be someone from the original writing group for each value statement, someone from the organization who is present for this job alone, or your consultant. It always helps to have someone type up the statements for distribution to the team after the session ends, to help facilitate further contemplation before the next development meeting.

The process of defining the value statement will take time. Give the group time to think, talk, brainstorm, and share. You will need to take breaks, and it may even be wise to have a meal or snacks available to the team during this process.

Once the team has gone as far as it can go with the first value definition, move onto the next one. Continue until the group has made suggestions, comments, and/or changes to all of the value statements. When all the values have been discussed, you might feel confident that they are complete. I would advise a cooling off period of a few days to let everyone think about the statements.

This sitting time allows for individuals to contemplate how they would talk about and use the value statement during their normal business routines.

Rule of Thumb:
The development team will do all they can to identify the values of the organization, if there is not a group consensus, the CEO, or ED will have final bottom-line decision-making power to define the value statement.

Congratulations! You have completed the work on the first part of your business's Vision statement: the value statement. After the initial value statement work is complete, the development team will move on to the task of developing the business's vision statement.

If the value statement development work moved along quickly, you may be prepared to move into developing your organization's vision statement, or you may want to take a break for a few days or a week to let the value statement sit. This break would be a good time to share the statement with other business partners and stakeholders in the company for input, before coming back together to move forward in developing the vision statement.

Rule of Thumb:

Even if the development team has come to a consensus, it is helpful to get feedback on your statement from other team members, board members, shareholders, and important community members. Ask them what they feel when they hear the value statement.

Chapter 6: Developing the Organization's Vision Statement

You are now ready to delve into your vision statement. It is good to remember during this entire development process that your value statement is open for discussion. It is a good idea to have an updated copy of the value statement in a visible place, as you work on your vision statement. It is also a good idea to make sure each of the development team members has a copy, electronic or paper, that they can refer to as they work on developing the next statement.

How to Develop the Vision Statement

The vision statement answers an important question: "What do we want to become in the future?" Just as with the value statement, this can appear to be a simple question on the surface. When you really think about the implications of answering such a question about your company, you will realize what you are developing is a mandate for how the company will operate in order to achieve this long-range objective. The vision statement asks us to be daring, creative, bold.

When you developed the value statement for your organization, you identified what the company stands for, how all team members work with each other and behave toward the company and community.

The value statement is the foundation upon which a company is built. Values are strong and long lasting; they do not change quickly, if at all. The vision statement asks you to leave what you know about your company behind, in order to expand the possibilities about what it can become in the future. We are all personally defined by our own ideas of what we are; organizations are no different. To develop the best vision statement for your organization, you must set aside current definitions of who you are. These can include the following:

- Your current markets and customers
- Your core competencies and capabilities
- Your geographic area
- Your history
- Your environment
- Your competitors
- Your industry
- Your governance (public, private, shareholders)
- Your level of leadership, excellence, service, and quality
- Your reputation
- Your public image
- What you are known for doing/being

You can expand your idea of who you are as an organization and, even more importantly, who you want to become. To do this, you must let go of how you currently think of your organization. Each of the items above is important, yet they can be traps as you want to grow and think bigger and bolder about the future. All the above are up for grabs as you develop your company's vision statement. Anything can change in the future. There may be some things you want to keep the same, but there are many times when you must change your current mindset to create a positive change and forward momentum for your organization.

In order to develop this new picture of our company, we have to escape our current reality for a bit. Aristotle is given credit for saying "The soul never thinks without a picture," so begin shaping the future of your company by creating a picture. When working with organizations that are developing their vision statement, I guide them through a visualization exercise about the future of their workplace. Visualization is a simple tool to let the mind see things, not as they are, but how we would like them to be. Visualization is used by a multitude of people in many work and social situations to see the outcome they desire.

One account is of Shaquille O'Neil. When he was having difficulty making free throw shots, Shaquille's trainers enlisted the help of a visualization coach to help him get past blocks he was having, while making this standard and very important game move.

First, Shaquille was advised to practice making free throws. He practiced, but in practice he continued to see failure. Shaquille was then instructed, in addition to his training, to add the practice of visualization. The exciting thing about visualization is, when practicing, you can see the desired outcome. Shaquille was advised to sit quietly in a comfortable environment with his eyes closed and envision himself making free throws. Not just seeing himself shooting the ball toward the basket but making the shot over and over. Seeing the ball going in the basket every time he threw it: swish, swish, swish. Visualization allows you to see only success. Because Shaquille was still seeing failure in his daily practices, he saw only minimal improvement in his free throw statistics. It was only when he spent more time visualizing successful free-throw shooting that his ability to make the ball go into the basket on a more regular basis improved.

There were also several interesting studies done with Olympic athletes. In one of the most well-known studies on creative visualization in sports, Russian scientists compared four groups of Olympic athletes in terms of their training schedules:

- Group 1 = 100% physical training.
- Group 2 - 75% physical training with 25% mental training.
- Group 3 - 50% physical training with 50% mental training.
- Group 4 - 25% physical training with 75% mental training.

Group 4, with 75% of their time devoted to mental training, performed the best. "The Soviets had discovered that mental images can act as a prelude to muscular impulses."

The power of mind over matter is proven in this and a multitude of other studies. The reason to include visualization in helping companies write their vision statement is, sometimes, the mind knows more than we give it credit for, and if given the opportunity, free from the constraints of our daily routines, our minds can show us new possibilities. In this situation, when we talk about making changes, those future possibilities are more likely to be freed.

> ### *Rule of Thumb:*
> Using visualization can free your everyday thinking and allow you to see more freely, with fresh eyes, the possibilities for your organization.

Prepare yourself; everyone who is on your development team should take part in this activity. You want as many ideas about what the organization can be in the future as possible. You may have someone read the visualization to you, or you may read it to yourself and then take time to think about all the possibilities. Most importantly, take your time. Do not rush through this exercise. It is the key to moving forward and writing the vision statement for your company.

- "It is 2035 (or pick a date at least five years from today's date). You are just arriving at work. What does the place you work at look like? Is it an office building? A factory? Your back bedroom?
- Walk in the front door. How is the customer area designed/decorated? Is there a counter, or is it a self-serve area? What is on the walls, floor, etc.?
- Are there greeters? What are their roles? What are they wearing? How do they greet you?

- Step into your work area. What functions take place here? How big is the space? How many employees help to get the work done?

- Is it a plant site? What equipment do you see? If it is an office, what is the physical set up? Offices? Cubicles? Open arrangement? What is the feel of the space? Clean? Warm? Inviting? Fun?

- Walk through the rest of the work areas. What do you see? What work is happening? How do things look? What sounds do you hear? Machines? People? What is on the walls, ceiling, and floor?

- Who oversees the work that is taking place? How are people interacting with one another?

- You are leaving the work site and as you open the door to go, a customer approaches. You hold the door for the customer, what does he say to you?"

If you are working with a development team, take a few minutes at the conclusion of the visualization exercise to discuss what each person saw.

Now that you have taken time to read over and spend time letting your subconscious brain do the work of seeing (visualizing) all of the possibilities the future holds for your organization, it is time to document your findings. Find your computer, tablet, or a piece of paper. It's time to write a press release.

Your organization has just been awarded the Sonia M. Keffer Excellence in Business award. (Everyone can dream, right?) Congratulations! You need to write a press release to inform the world of your success and just what you attribute it to. Take a few minutes to write your press release and be sure to include the name of the organization, where it is located, who is the current CEO or ED, and to what do you attribute your success over the last decade, which resulted in your receiving this prestigious award.

Taking the time to write down your successes in this format is a great way to bring what you saw in your mind's eye into a workable format. Really think about what you just visualized. This is not about reality. This is not about how we make it happen? It's not about the constraints of time and money. It is about the possibility of what your company can become in the future, not in the next week, the next month, or even the next year, but over the next several years with consistent and persistent effort by all parties.

After all team members have written their press releases, take time to have them all read theirs aloud. Have someone take notes about major new ideas or trends the group wants to remember. Post these where everyone can see them.

It is now time to begin to think about writing a vision statement for your company. Just like writing the value statement, it helps to have some examples of other companies' vision statements. Here are some:

Warby Parker
"We believe buying glasses should be easy and fun."

John F. Kennedy
"A Man on the Moon by the End of the Decade."

Lowe's
"We will provide customer-valued solutions with the best prices, products, and services to make Lowe's the first choice for home improvement."

Southwest Airlines, Inc.
"To be the world's most loved, most efficient, and most profitable airline."

Starbucks
"To establish Starbucks as the premier purveyor of the finest coffee in the world while maintaining our uncompromising principles while we grow."

SONY

1950s: Become the Company most known for changing the worldwide poor-quality image of Japanese products.

Current: "To be a company that inspires and fulfills your curiosity. Our unlimited passion for technology, content, services, and relentless pursuit of innovation drives us to deliver ground-breaking new excitement and entertainment in ways that only Sony can."

Oregon Shakespeare Festival

"We envision the Oregon Shakespeare Festival as a creative environment where artists and audiences from around the world know they can explore opportunities for transformational experiences through the power of theatre."

The goal of the vision statement is to be a concise, succinct, simple statement of your organization's shared hopes and dreams for the future. It should honor your value statement, meaning, the vision should take the values of the organization into account while building on them, creating forward movement. The vision statement should excite employees to keep moving forward in their daily work, but with a well-defined path for future decision-making.

> **Rule of Thumb:**
> Another way of thinking about the vision statement is a "call to action" for the entire organization.

Now that everyone on the development team has visualized the future of the organization, written a press release about the successes of the company, and seen examples of other's vision statements, it is time to write the vision statement.

Once again, here is a check list of how best to divide your development team into smaller work groups.

- Break the larger group into smaller groups of 2-5 people. (When dividing your development team members up, keep in mind the need for maximum freedom to brainstorm and minimum interpersonal conflict.)
- Provide tools/resources for brainstorming (note paper, flip chart, markers, and dictionary/ thesaurus).
- Provide historical information on values, value statements, vision statements, and mission statements.
- Give a time frame and clear objectives for the exercise.

- Remind participants of guidelines for brainstorming. (No bad/wrong ideas, write down everything, generate as many ideas as possible and evaluate them later).

When the groups have created their draft vision statements, bring everyone back together. Have each group share their vision statements with the larger development team. Again, you can appoint a group leader to facilitate the small group sharing or have the hired consultant lead this part. The draft statements should be posted, so everyone in the group can see them clearly. Take time to let each group share their statements and explain their meanings to the organization and how they relate to the value statement, as well as to the future of the organization itself.

After each of the groups has shared their draft vision statement, open a larger group discussion about each statement. Let individuals talk about their ideas, what they like from each draft and how they think it will impact passion and action throughout the entire organization. This discussion and brainstorming session may go on for several minutes to an hour. If it seems that the development team needs longer, either give them a break and return to the work, or table the discussion, making sure each party has a copy of all of the materials and agree on a next meeting date to continue the discussion and come to a consensus on the vision statement.

You may find the development team quickly comes to consensus. This has been my experience with several companies. Once the value statement is in place, the vision becomes clear rather quickly and without much effort or argument. Most people know what the big goal is and enjoy the opportunity to state it powerfully.

Rule of Thumb:
Discussions about the vision statement may end up being a discussion of semantics or word meaning. If the conversation starts to get too intense or heated, call for a break. Some debate is good and needed to come to the best conclusion, but sometimes it can get personal quickly. Work hard to make sure that everyone's self-esteem is left in-tact through this process.

Either way, whether the development team comes to consensus easily or needs more time, don't print anything yet. Take time to sit with the statements. Now you have a value statement and a draft vision statement. Just as with the value statement, take up to a week to ponder the statements and to share them with other important people in the company to get feedback.

When you meet next, the development team will come to consensus on the vision statement and move on to developing the organization's mission statement.

Congratulations on your work so far. In the next chapter, we will focus on what the mission statement is and some ideas for you to use as you develop this concept for your organization.

Chapter 7: Developing the Organization's Mission Statement

Hopefully, as you are beginning this chapter, you have already developed at least draft versions of value and vision statements for your company. If you are just reading through, that is great too. These "how to" chapters can give you a head start on how to begin developing the value, vision, and mission statements for your non-profit or for-profit organization. These statements make up the larger company Vision that allows you to share your total image of your company with both internal and external team members, shareholders, customers, and supportive community members. As we move forward, let us assume that you have already spent some time developing your value and vision statements.

Are your Value and Vision Statements complete?

When you reconvene to continue your work, you will want to revisit your value and vision statements. Does the development group still agree the value statement represents the company well? Do the statements state simply, yet completely, what the company stands for?

Is it easy for the reader to understand what your company is all about and what they can expect when doing business with you by reading your value statement? Are there slight changes that the group wants to make? Feel free to do so, posting them on the wall, so everyone can contemplate possible changes. Don't feel pressured to make changes; only know changes at this stage are still possible.

Think about the vision statement the group worked on during your last session. Is the group ready to come to consensus on the statement? Does it represent where the organization wants to be in the next five to ten years? Is it inspiring? Does it make you want to set actionable goals to create forward momentum within the organization? This would be a good time to review any feedback that the development group may have received from others regarding the vision statement. As ideas are shared, post them on the wall. Allow time for the ideas to set in before trying to reach consensus. If the group is ready, take the next step and agree. For now, the statement developed by the group will be the "working" vision statement for the organization.

How to Develop the Mission Statement

If the value statement asks what your organization stands for and the vision statement asks you to identify your organization's shared hopes and dreams for the future, then what does the mission statement ask? This statement asks why we exist, who we serve, and what we produce. In an earlier chapter, we discussed that the mission statement helps drive day-to-day activity. What are we doing daily to live our values and to move closer to achieving our vision? Very often it happens that the work you have done up to this point, in many organizations, is called the mission statement. There is nothing inherently wrong with this; however, by using the values and/or vision statement as your mission, you miss out on answering the questions about why you exist, who you serve, and what you produce. The answers to these questions and the mission statement that you develop include very important information that your internal team members, external customers, and shareholders, need to know so they can understand how your company works on a daily basis.

The Role of the Mission Statement

The importance of the mission statement is in the role it plays in keeping the company functioning to full capacity as well as moving confidently forward.

According to *Strategic Planning for New and Emerging Businesses* by authors Fry, Stoner, and Weinzimmer, the role of the mission statement is two-fold.

1. The mission statement acts as a communication tool, letting those internally and externally know the company's plan, as well as, clarifying the company's vision and establishing each person's role in the company's future.

2. The mission statement commits the CEO, ED, and other leaders to the strategy and philosophy outlined in the statement and should result in buy-in from all employees and shareholders.

For many businesses, the mission statement is the only published part of the company Vision. Typically, the value and vision statements are for internal use only. You may choose to do the same with your statements, feeling that they are more personal to the organization. If that is the case, the mission statement needs to encompass the feel of the value and vision statements, while explaining the simple specifics of what you do.

Here are some guidelines to keep in mind about mission statements.

Your mission statement should:

- Be clear and understandable.
- Be brief enough to keep in mind.
- Specify a direction.
- Include a description of your preferred outcomes.
- Reflect your distinct competency as an organization.
- Be broad enough to allow flexibility in implementation, but not so broad that it lacks focus.
- Serve as a guide for decision making.
- Reflect company values and vision.
- Be achievable and challenging, yet realistic.
- Serve as a source of energy for you and the organization.

The above list is a guide. Some of the items may seem contradictory, yet they provide a good checklist to reference as the development team begins writing the mission statement.

> ### *Rule of Thumb:*
> Even though you are writing your value, vision, and mission statements, you may choose to only publish your mission statement. If this is the case, make sure that the mission encompasses some of the feel and words of the value and vision statements.

Mission Statement Examples

You will notice greater differences in how companies write their mission statements versus their value and vision statements. This is because some companies do not have separate value and vision statements and try to include all that information in one statement. By using the methods outlined in this book, you have the luxury of keeping your mission simplified, knowing that you have your value and vision outlined separately. Let these statements get your creativity flowing. My advice, as always, is to take what you can use from these statements, in terms of structure and word usage, as you create your organization's mission statement.

Ben & Jerry's

Ben & Jerry's is founded on and dedicated to a sustainable corporate concept of linked prosperity. Central to the Mission of Ben & Jerry's is the belief that all three parts of its mission must thrive equally in a manner that commands deep respect for individuals inside and outside the Company and supports the communities of which they are part.

TED

TED is on a mission to discover and spread ideas that spark imagination, embrace possibility and catalyze impact. Our organization is devoted to curiosity, reason, wonder and the pursuit of knowledge — without an agenda. We welcome people from every discipline and culture who seek a deeper understanding of the world and connection with others, and we invite everyone to engage with ideas and activate them in your community.

Whole Foods Market

Our purpose is to nourish people and the planet. We're a purpose-driven company that aims to set the standards of excellence for food retailers. Quality is a state of mind at Whole Foods Market.

67

Curtis and Associates, Inc.

Curtis and Associates, Inc. will have an international impact on reducing poverty and unemployment. Through our efforts millions of people will have higher self-esteem, higher hopes for the future and jobs that will enhance their self-sufficiency. Governments will save millions of dollars through the efforts of our company.

Our goal is to motivate people to value and to succeed in securing self-sufficiency. We will do all we can to support and sustain each other as we work together to accomplish this goal.

Lowe's

Lowe's is in the business of providing products to help customers build, improve, and enjoy their homes. Our goal is to out-service the competition and be our customers' 1st Choice Store for these products.

Sony

To be a company that inspires and fulfills your curiosity. Our unlimited passion for technology, content, services, and relentless pursuit of innovation drives us to deliver ground-breaking new excitement and entertainment in ways that only Sony can.

Fashion Cleaners

Our company exists to provide the highest level of consistent workmanship in the care of garments and household items.

We believe in providing a superior valued service in a harmonious and growth-oriented environment.

Our goal is to be the leading garment care company in the Omaha metro area, serving our customers through continuous training and honest communication.

Warby Parker

To offer designer eyewear at a revolutionary price while leading the way for socially conscious businesses.

Burger King

Burger King is flame-broiled burgers, fries and soft drinks at a good value served quickly and consistently by friendly people, in clean surroundings.

Southwest Airlines

Dedication to the highest quality of customer service delivered with a sense of warmth, friendliness, individual pride, and company spirit.

Metropolitan Community College, Omaha, Nebraska

Our Mission at Metropolitan Community College is to serve our community with distinction. We are a role model in higher education. We will deliver:

- Quality Learning Opportunities.
- Lifelong educational programs.
- Services that support personal and professional enrichment and training.
- Programs and services which stimulate economic and workforce development.
- Courses and programs which provide a transferable path to baccalaureate institutions.
- Career/vocational education supporting business and economic partnerships.
- A positive learning environment that promotes student success.

Omaha Public Schools

The mission of the Omaha Public Schools is to provide educational opportunities which enable all students to achieve their highest potential.

Educational Aims

1. High Student Achievement
2. Safe and Secure Learning Environment
3. Professional Work Force
4. Partnerships
5. Effective and Efficient use of District Resources

Educational Equity

Aligned with the mission of the Omaha Public Schools is the commitment to educational equity for all students, staff, and patrons of the school system. In all places and in all activities of the Omaha Public Schools, it is expected that every individual will be treated in a fair and equitable manner. All conduct will reflect a belief in the dignity and value of each person regardless of the individual's race, color, religion, sex, sexual orientation, national origin, disability, age, marital status, citizenship status, or economic status.

Oregon Shakespeare Festival

The Mission Statement of the Oregon Shakespeare Festival is to create fresh and bold interpretations of classic and contemporary plays in repertoire, shaped by the diversity of our American culture, using Shakespeare as our standard and inspiration.

These examples represent just a sample of all the types of mission statements that companies have. I agree with the sentiment of Quigley, in *Vision: How leaders Develop it, Share it, Sustain it,* that having different mission statements only show that what works for one company does not work for all. The most important thing in a mission statement is that "…each organization should select the elements most appropriate for them."

How to Develop the Mission Statement

In all the years I have been helping organizations develop their company Vision, the simplest method for creating the mission statement I have discovered is a fill in the blank format. After all the work you and the development team have done to this point, this may feel like a rip-off, but I assure you it is because of all the work done on the value and vision statements which will allow developing the mission statement to be this uncomplicated. The format of the mission statement that I like is:

"The mission of _____ is to provide_____ to_____ in order to_____."

An example of what this looks like when it is complete is from the Academic Support Division of Metropolitan Community College in Omaha, Nebraska:

The mission of Academic Support is to provide assistance with building academic skills, conducting research, and utilizing resources for the college community, in order to foster learning and empower individuals to achieve their goals.

Since I worked with this group personally, I can tell you, as simple and succinct as this statement appears, it took the development team eight hours of intense work to formulate the statement. Even then, it was scrutinized, and slight changes were made by the bottom-line decision makers.

The way to make the most of this simple process is to break it down into smaller pieces. Rather than dividing the development teams in groups to tackle the entire statement at once, begin by asking the smaller groups (Please review the ideas on how to set up smaller work groups in the resource section of this book) to start with the first blank, the one that answers, "The mission of_____." Or, in other words, who are we?

Now, this one may be very easy for your company, or you may really want to think about your name, as the Academic Support team did. They completely changed the name of their department, as a part of this process from Student Services to Academic Support. It may seem a small change, but this team, whose main areas are tutoring centers, computer labs, and libraries, wanted a name to describe more fully what they do to support students and their college community.

After all participants in the small groups have had time to share their ideas for the first blank, bring the larger group together and share ideas just as you have done with the value and vision statements. Perhaps, a consensus will be reached, and perhaps not. You may end up with a short list of ideas you want to hold onto, as you progress through the mission statement development process. From there, move on to the second blank in the mission statement, "…is to provide."

In other words, what do you do? Have the small groups brainstorm for fifteen to thirty minutes, and then, have everyone share and discuss their ideas. Continue through the statement blanks. The next blank "…to…" refers to whom you provide your products or services, in other words your customers. Who are they, and how do you refer to them? Is that a correct term? Would you like to change it? Here's your chance. The fourth blank in the mission statement is "…in order to…," or to achieve what? This may be different for non-profits and for-profit organizations, but all organizations are in business for some reason. What is yours?

Rule of Thumb:
Perhaps, a consensus will be reached and, perhaps, not. Certainly, you will end up with a short list of ideas that you want to hold onto as you progress through the mission statement development process.

Your development group should be able to work through the mission statement in one session; however, you may break it into two sessions, if that feels more manageable or as schedules dictate.

Just as in prior development sessions, you may leave the session feeling confident you have completed your mission statement, or you may end the session feeling you have many great ideas and would like to take more time to flesh them out, either by thinking about them more or by gathering other important people's input. In either case, I would suggest you let the statements sit for a few days, and then, get the development team back together, either in person, or via a conference call, to share new thoughts and determine if you are ready to reach consensus on your statement.

I hope it's clear that it is important to make these statements yours – a reflection of your organization, not an imitation of some other business. They are unique to you, what you stand for, what you hope to achieve by being in business, and what you do on a daily basis in your company to make the world a better place.

The development process is unique to each organization. You may move quickly through the development steps, or you may choose to take more time. Either way is fine. The outcome is more important than the method. What you want are statements that represent your company in the very best way possible and that you will proudly share with team members, shareholders, and the larger community.

Rule of Thumb:

Remember that the statements that you and the development team create are yours. They represent your company, what you stand for, what you do, and ultimately what you want to become. Take time to make sure that each statement has your company's stamp of individuality on it.

Chapter 8: What does the Organization do with the Mission, Vision, and Value Statements?
Share it!

By the time you have reached this chapter, you may have written your mission, vision, and value statements, but you may still be wondering what they can do for your organization, aside from hanging them on the wall so customers and clients can see them in a lovely frame as they enter your office. For many companies, this is what the Vision is used for: decoration. These companies, well-meaning with great products and services, think that is all there is to it. A company Vision is so much more.

It is not only to be displayed, but also to be shared. Make sure everyone knows what you are about. The company Vision encompasses three statements, which tell the world about your organization from the inside out.

1. Value Statement—answering what your company stands for.
2. Vision Statement—answering where you want the company to be in five to ten years. And,
3. Mission Statement—answering why the company exists.

Everyone you do business with and everyone you want to do business with needs to and wants to know these things about you.

Aside from placing a lovely copy on the wall in your office, how can you spread the word? Start with places you already share information about your company.

- Have it printed on your letterhead.
- Have it on all your company's printed marketing materials (i.e., brochures, flyers, etc.).
- Make sure it is visible on your company website's front page and have a link to it that includes more detailed information. This is where you can also list your value statement and vision statement if you wish.
- Make sure it is on your company's Facebook, LinkedIn, and other social media sites.
- Whenever you issue a press release, include at least your organization's mission statement, as well.

As mentioned earlier, you may choose to make your entire company Vision public, or you may choose simply to publish the mission statement.

> **Rule of Thumb:**
> Your Vision is meant to tell the world what your company is all about. Share your statement in as many ways as possible to get the word out.

I understand you may create a tagline or memorable quote you will use in your marketing/ advertising, and this tagline may encompass some part of your company's mission statement, yet it is not a substitute for your mission statement.

If you want the world to know who you are, what you do, and who you do it for, then spread the word by sharing your company Vision in writing and verbally, as often as you can.

Let your Mission Lead Your Company

Now that you understand sharing your mission statement everywhere and with everyone is of vital importance to your business's success, you now need to have it do its job for your company.

What do I mean?

As we have discussed, an organizational Vision is not just a pretty wall decoration, it has a job to do. It's an important job. I fear many company leaders feel once the initial writing of the mission statement is done, everyone can just get back to work.

When this happens, and it happens far too often, a disconnect is created between the work a company does and what the company started out wanting to create, when it was originally founded.

According to *Strategic Planning for New and Emerging Business*, "The mission statement (Vision) provides a central focus and unifying drive for the business within its future." The Vision needs not only to be in front of each current and potential customer each and every day, but also in front of each company leader and team member. This is not accomplished by having a copy hanging in every office, hallway, restroom, and computer sleep screen, which are great ideas, but by having the Vision be the starting point of every team meeting and discussion about business direction.

When an organization is not guided by its Vision, it can easily get off track and begin pursuing things that don't align with who they said they are and who they wanted to be. One of the first jobs I had out of college was for a consulting firm. This organization provided contract training for state and local governments all across the country. At each and every team meeting, we would start by reciting the company's mission statement and guiding principles. By doing this, we were reminded of why we existed, what we did, who we did it for, and how we did it. This made it easier to say, "Yes," to some ideas about business procedures and new business growth as well as saying, "No," to other ideas that did not meet our mission.

Does this sound limiting? I suppose it could. Yet, I would argue that for a new or newer business, it is critically important to keep growing in the direction you intended. The danger is growing too big too fast, and before long no one knows what the company is about anymore.

> **Rule of Thumb:**
> Let your company Vision guide your business decisions.

Mergers, acquisitions, adding new products and services because we overheard someone say we should add them are not necessarily the best reason to do something. As you may have already discovered, everyone is going to have opinions about how you can improve your business. It is ultimately up to you and your leadership team to decide whether that big new idea is the right big idea. If it is, great. Act. Move. Grow. However, it is wise to double-check your vision statement and ask yourself the hard questions about what you want your company to be in the future before making major changes or decisions. Remember to let your value and vision statements be your guide. After doing your research, you may decide to consider it later, but not now.

Whenever there is a decision to be made about business direction and operation, consult your Vision. Let it do its job. Let it help you grow your company with the consistency and integrity you had in mind when you started it.

Use It to Guide all Human Resource Decisions

If you are using your Vision as a guide for making all business decisions, it stands to reason you would also use it to guide your decisions about how to interact with team members through human resource policies.

How does this work?

As an example, I would like to showcase a company I had the privilege of assisting in the development of their mission, vision, and value statements. Fashion Cleaners/Omaha Lace Laundry is a dry cleaning and home accessory cleaning company with five locations in the Omaha metropolitan area. To highlight just one aspect of their Vision, their mission statement says,

"Our Company exists to provide the highest level of consistent workmanship in the care of garments and household items. We believe in providing a superior valued service in a harmonious and growth-oriented environment. Our goal is to be the leading garment care company in the Omaha metro area, serving our customers through continuous training and honest communication."

As you can see, they talk about the company they will be if you work for them. They share how they aim to treat employees and what employees (team members) should expect in return from Fashion Cleaners. This company was already several decades old when it decided to revisit the mission statement, so some of the items in the mission statement above were the way they were already operating, and some emerged, as they considered how they wanted to enhance who they are.

There are many human resource functions which must take place for a company to run well and continue meeting its Vision. For more on aligning human resources processes to your Vision, check out *A Guide to Peak Performance Through People* by Todd A. Conkright, another *Rule of Thumb* author. Some which need to be Vision driven are Job Descriptions, Hiring Practices, Employee Promotions, and Employee Evaluations. If we start by keeping our human resource procedures driven by the company Vision, then many future business decisions will be easier.

Let's start with job descriptions. Having a description of the specific job duties and required experiences is a must for each job within a business. I understand if you are a one-person business or a two-or-three-member partnership, you may feel this is difficult to do. Everyone just jumps in and does what needs to be done.

However, even in those very small organizations, I would suggest you create job descriptions, not to keep people stuck in certain roles, but in order to help minimize conflict as things grow. It's almost a joke now, but each job description usually ends with "and, duties as assigned." What that really says is, "I agree to chip in and help out the business in any way I can when my extra effort is needed." Therefore, job descriptions can be made for any business, no matter how many employees there are currently.

When writing job descriptions, refer to the mission, vision, and value statements. These statements are the core of who your company is, and they should be doing their job of helping you run and grow your business.

If Fashion Cleaners (mentioned above) was writing a job description for a general garment care team member, some of the thing's executives may want to include after referring to their mission statement might be:

- Attends all company and profession required trainings/in-services.
- Follows all garment care procedures as established by Fashion Cleaners.
- Takes pride in work produced, always keeping the customer in mind.
- Is honest and dependable.
- Will submit to all work required drug screenings.

- Works to maintain positive relationships with team members and customers.
- Communicates with team members in polite and honest ways to share important information.
- Follows company procedures for dealing with team and customer conflict.
- Adheres to the mission, vision, and value statements of Fashion Cleaners/Omaha Lace Laundry.

Of course, there will be other job specific requirements and duties listed in the job description. This initial list of requirements creates a roadmap to keep the leadership team on track, when looking for the most qualified person for the job.

Rule of Thumb:
Consult your mission, vision, and value statements when developing job descriptions.

Take some time to look over the job descriptions for your business. Are there elements of your mission, vision, and value statements present in each description? If not, take the time to add them, you will not be disappointed.

Second, let's talk about hiring. Almost every company hires employees as it grows. It is easy to look online or purchase a book or even borrow from another company application formats and interview questions, yet it may be a waste of time. If you have taken the time to create a job description for each position within your company, then you are already one step ahead. Use your Vision-driven job description, as you write your advertisement for a new employee. List the necessary duties in the description. This makes the job advertisement the first screening tool. You can check all applications and resumes that come to you for the job against the original advertisement, as well as the job description before inviting a prospective candidate in for an interview.

Nothing replaces the in-person interview in the hiring process. If, however, you are only asking the basic interview questions every other business is asking, how do you know if you are hiring the right person for your organization? The simple answer is you don't. Once again, by using your mission, vision, and value statements, we can create a business-specific list of interview questions which will help you hire the exact right person. Going back to our Vision-driven job description, we can create questions for each position that will help you understand how each candidate will use their education, past experiences, and personality in your work environment.

Let's look at our Fashion Cleaners example again, and let's look at just a couple of interview question options for a garment care team member.

- Tell me about a time when you had to follow certain procedures to accomplish a goal?
- Was that difficult for you? Or easy? Why?
- Give me an example of a time when you were very proud of your work?
- Tell me about a time when you experienced conflict with a team member. What happened? What did you do? How did the situation conclude?
- Do you have a personal mission statement or a set of core values that you live by?

By taking the time to create business and job specific interview questions, you are developing a significant screening tool for hiring new team members. If you hire people who are already in synch with your company's Vision, then training them and having them assimilate into your company culture will be much easier, and the company work can move ahead at a faster pace because the learning curve is not as steep.

> **Rule of Thumb:**
> Another use for the Vision statement is to use it as a guide when developing interview questions. We all want team members who assimilate well into our culture and using your Vision will help you understand who would be a good fit for your team.

Remember to use developed job descriptions and position-specific interview questions when promoting from within. Just because a team member does a good job in his current position does not mean he is automatically suited to be promoted to a new one with more responsibility.

Lastly, let's discuss Employee Evaluations. This is an area many companies struggle with. Many of us, as business leaders and owners, have our own issues with how to give feedback in constructive ways. Many of us fear the intense emotion which can accompany giving team members their "Annual Review." I understand these fears. They come from how we were given feedback in the past, our own ability to deal with emotion and conflict, how we were taught to (or not taught to) give feedback, and perhaps, most importantly, the syndrome of "too little too late."

Many organizations wait until an annual or semiannual review to give team members any positive or critical feedback, making these events intense and confrontational.

What can we do?

I hope with what we have already covered in this chapter you can see how easy it will be to create a job specific Vision-driven evaluation. By going back to the job description, you can almost turn each bullet point into an evaluation item. There may be some specific goals that you will want to add to the evaluation form and give some space for the team member to write a self-evaluation of his work accomplishments and areas of needed improvement during the period reviewed. You will use these to create new goals for the team members, and the team.

There are many ways to structure an employee evaluation form, from rating scales to written comments. Whichever you choose, using the job description as the basis for the areas that will be evaluated will make the entire process simpler and less subjective.

Now, you have created a useable evaluation tool. My only suggestion would be to make it available to each team member. Part of new hire training should be a review of how the values and mission intersect with the specific role the person is filling.

They should know how they will be held accountable for living out the Vision of the company. Once you've done this, you can reinforce it by "catching" them living out the values and acknowledging or rewarding that behavior. The more frequently you provide both formal and informal feedback to employees, the more you can reinforce alignment with what is important to the organization. We all want to do our best and have it noticed. Start noticing, and you will start getting what you desire. It's much harder to hide unsatisfactory work if there is a discussion between my boss and I once a month versus just once or twice a year.

Rule of Thumb:
If you have used your Vision statement to write job descriptions for each member of your team, then you have already done the work of creating an understandable and usable evaluation form.

Using your Vision to help create necessary human resource documents and processes can effectively enhance your organization's ability to hire and retain the right team members in the right positions, which can help your company grow and allow team members to feel fully engaged in their work.

Chapter 9: Conclusion

As a consultant and trainer for over twenty years, I am constantly reminding team leaders and team members of how important it is to rely upon the company's mission, vision, and value statements to guide them in their day-to-day work, as well as in their long-term strategic planning and goal setting.

Living out an organization's Vision is the job of everyone within the company. Of course, all individuals have their to-do list of daily tasks that they must work through, but it is ultimately everyone's job to reflect the company's values while achieving the mission and aspiring to the vision set out by the company's leadership.

You are an entrepreneur, business owner, and a leader. It is your job to ensure the Vision you outline in your value, vision, and mission statements does not get lost in the everyday details. You must make them the mandate: a compass that will guide you as you operate your company from its very core relationships to creating the future you had in mind the day you started the business. Yours is a challenging position.

Everyone is looking to you for direction, insight, feedback, and inspiration, all great reasons to keep your Vision in the fore of your everyday thinking.

Your Vision is not just a set of pretty words for shareholders and potential board members; it is what you do and what you want to accomplish. Keep your statements, values, vision, and mission, close at hand. Look at them every day. Yes, every day. Use them in your leadership role to guide you in leading your people and leading your business. Remember:

- **What do you believe in? (Value statement)**
- **Where do you want to be in the future? (Vision statement)**
- **Why do you exist? (Mission statement)**

These three questions, and the answers you have to them, whether written and published at this point, or not, are the key to your business success. Nothing else will take you where you want to go.

As Thoreau said, "Go confidently in the direction of your dreams." Having a solid company Vision will make you better equipped to handle the challenges that may arise on your journey and better equipped to celebrate the successes that will come from your effort. The purpose of this book is to make the development of your company Vision statement as understandable and easily manageable as possible. I hope I have helped you understand the importance of having value, vision, and mission statements for your business and how to develop each one of the statements in a straightforward manner, as well as, how the statements can help you make running your business as successful as possible.

Appendix 1: Value statement word list
Copyright 2008 - Living More, LLC

1. Abundance
2. Acceptance
3. Accessibility
4. Accomplishment
5. Accuracy
6. Achievement
7. Acknowledgement
8. Activeness
9. Adaptability
10. Adoration
11. Adroitness
12. Adventure
13. Affection
14. Affluence
15. Aggressiveness
16. Agility
17. Alertness
18. Altruism
19. Ambition
20. Amusement
21. Anticipation
22. Appreciation
23. Approachability
24. Articulacy
25. Assertiveness
26. Assurance
27. Attentiveness
28. Attractiveness
29. Audacity
30. Availability
31. Awareness
32. Awe
33. Balance
34. Beauty
35. Being the best
36. Belonging
37. Benevolence
38. Bliss
39. Boldness
40. Bravery
41. Brilliance
42. Buoyancy
43. Calmness
44. Camaraderie
45. Candor
46. Capability
47. Care
48. Carefulness
49. Celebrity
50. Certainty
51. Challenge
52. Charity
53. Charm
54. Chastity
55. Cheerfulness
56. Clarity

57. Cleanliness
58. Clear Mindedness
59. Cleverness
60. Closeness
61. Comfort
62. Commitment
63. Compassion
64. Completion
65. Composure
66. Concentration
67. Confidence
68. Conformity
69. Congruency
70. Connection
71. Consciousness
72. Consistency
73. Contentment
74. Continuity
75. Contribution
76. Control
77. Conviction
78. Conviviality
79. Coolness
80. Cooperation
81. Cordiality
82. Correctness
83. Courage
84. Courtesy

85. Craftiness
86. Creativity
87. Credibility
88. Cunning
89. Curiosity
90. Daring
91. Decisiveness
92. Decorum
93. Deference
94. Delight
95. Dependability
96. Depth
97. Desire
98. Determination
99. Devotion
100. Devoutness
101. Dexterity
102. Dignity
103. Diligence
104. Direction
105. Directness
106. Discipline
107. Discovery
108. Discretion
109. Diversity
110. Dominance
111. Dreaming
112. Drive

113. Duty
114. Dynamism
115. Eagerness
116. Economy
117. Ecstasy
118. Education
119. Effectiveness
120. Efficiency
121. Elation
122. Elegance
123. Empathy
124. Encouragement
125. Endurance
126. Energy
127. Enjoyment
128. Entertainment
129. Enthusiasm
130. Excellence
131. Excitement
132. Exhilaration
133. Expectancy
134. Expediency
135. Experience
136. Expertise
137. Exploration
138. Expressiveness
139. Extravagance
140. Extroversion
141. Exuberance
142. Fairness
143. Faith
144. Fame
145. Family
146. Fascination
147. Fashion
148. Fearlessness
149. Ferocity
150. Fidelity
152. Financial independence
153. Firmness
154. Fitness
155. Flexibility
156. Flow
157. Fluency
158. Focus
159. Fortitude
160. Frankness
161. Freedom
162. Friendliness
163. Frugality
164. Fun
165. Gallantry
166. Generosity
167. Gentility
168. Giving
169. Grace

170. Gratitude

171. Gregariousness

172. Growth

173. Guidance

174. Happiness

175. Harmony

176. Health

177. Heart

178. Helpfulness

179. Heroism

180. Holiness

181. Honesty

182. Honor

183. Hopefulness

184. Hospitality

185. Humility

186. Humor

187. Hygiene

188. Imagination

189. Impact

190. Impartiality

191. Independence

192. Industry

193. Ingenuity

194. Inquisitiveness

195. Insightfulness

196. Inspiration

197. Integrity

198. Intelligence

199. Intensity

200. Intimacy

201. Intrepidness

202. Introversion

203. Intuition

204. Intuitiveness

205. Inventiveness

206. Investing

207. Joy

208. Judiciousness

209. Justice

210. Keenness

211. Kindness

212. Knowledge

213. Leadership

214. Learning

215. Liberation

216. Liberty

217. Liveliness

218. Logic

219. Longevity

220. Looking good

221. Love

222. Loyalty

223. Majesty

224. Making a difference

225. Mastery

226. Maturity

227. Meekness

228. Mellowness

254. Philanthropy

255. Piety

256. Playfulness

229. Meticulousness
230. Mindfulness
231. Modesty
232. Motivation
233. Mysteriousness
234. Nature
235. Neatness
236. Nerve
237. Obedience
238. Open-mindedness
239. Openness
240. Optimism
241. Order
242. Organization
243. Originality
244. Outlandishness
245. Outrageousness
246. Passion
247. Peace
248. Perceptiveness
249. Perfection
250. Perkiness
251. Perseverance
252. Persistence
253. Persuasiveness
257. Pleasantness
258. Pleasure
259. Poise
260. Polish
261. Popularity
262. Potency
263. Power
264. Practicality
265. Pragmatism
266. Precision
267. Preparedness
268. Presence
269. Privacy
270. Proactivity
271. Professionalism
272. Prosperity
273. Prudence
274. Punctuality
275. Purity
276. Realism
277. Reason
278. Reasonableness
279. Recognition
280. Recreation
281. Refinement

282. Reflection
283. Relaxation
284. Reliability
285. Religiousness
286. Resilience
287. Resolution
288. Resolve
289. Resourcefulness
290. Respect
291. Rest
292. Restraint
293. Reverence
294. Richness
295. Rigor
296. Ritual
297. Sacredness
298. Sacrifice
299. Sagacity
300. Saintliness
301. Sanguinity
302. Satisfaction
303. Security
304. Self-control
305. Selflessness
306. Self-reliance
307. Sensitivity
308. Sensuality
309. Serenity

310. Service
311. Sexuality
312. Sharing
313. Shrewdness
314. Significance
315. Silence
316. Silliness
317. Simplicity
318. Sincerity
319. Skillfulness
320. Solidarity
321. Solitude
322. Soundness
323. Speed
324. Spirit
325. Spirituality
326. Spontaneity
327. Spunk
328. Stability
329. Stealth
330. Stillness
331. Strength
332. Structure
333. Success
334. Support
335. Supremacy
336. Surprise
337. Sympathy

338. Synergy
339. Teamwork
340. Temperance
341. Thankfulness
342. Thoroughness
343. Thoughtfulness
344. Thrift
345. Tidiness
346. Timeliness
347. Traditionalism
348. Tranquility
349. Transcendence
350. Trust
351. Trustworthiness
352. Truth
353. Understanding
354. Unflappability
355. Uniqueness
356. Unity
357. Usefulness
358. Utility
359. Valor
360. Variety
361. Victory
362. Vigor
363. Virtue
364. Vision
365. Vitality
366. Vivacity
367. Warmth
368. Watchfulness
369. Wealth
370. Willfulness
371. Willingness
372. Winning
373. Wisdom
374. Wittiness
375. Wonder
376. Youthfulness
377. Zeal

Appendix 2
How to separate your development team into smaller work groups

- Break the larger group into smaller groups of 2-5 people. (When dividing your development team members up, keep in mind the need for maximum freedom to brainstorm and minimum interpersonal conflict.)
- Provide tools/resources for brainstorming (note paper, flip chart, markers, dictionary/ thesaurus)
- Provide historical information on, value statements, vision statements, and mission statements.
- Give a time frame and clear objectives for the exercise.
- Remind participants of guidelines for brainstorming. (No bad/wrong ideas, write down everything, generate as many ideas as possible and evaluate later).

Bibliography

(The author notes that all webpages were active as of March 2023)

Ben and Jerry's Homemade Ice Cream. N.p., n.d. Web. 8 May 2012. <http://www.benjerry.com/http://>.

Burger King. N.p., n.d. Web. 8 May 2012. <http://www. bk.com/>.

Celestial Seasonings 100% Natural Teas. N.p., n.d. Web. 8 May 2012. <http://www.celestialseasonings.com>.

Concord Mediation Center. N.p., n.d. Web. 8 May 2012. <http://www.concordmediationcenter.com/>.

Covey, Stephen M.R., and Rebecca R. Merrill. *The Speed of Trust*. New York: Free Press-Simon, 2006. Print.

Covey, Stephen R. *Principle-Centered Leadership*. 3rd ed. New York: Fireside-Simon, 1992. Print.

Cummins, William, and Robert Scaglione. *Karate of Okinawa: Building Warrior Spirit*. New York City: Person to Person, 1993. N. pag. Print.

Fashion Cleaners. N.p., n.d. Web. 9 May 2012. <http://www.fashioncleaners.com/>.

Fry, Fred L, Charles Stoner, and Laurence Weinzimmer. *Strategic Planning for New & Emerging Businesses: A Consulting Approach*. Chicago: Dearborn TradeKaplan, 1999. Print.

Haines, Stephen G. *Successful Strategic Planning*. Menlo Park: Crisp, 1995. Print.

Heinz. N.p., n.d. Web. 9 May 2012. <http://www.heinz. com/>.

Herman Miller. N.p., n.d. Web. 9 May 2012.
  <http:// www.hermanmiller.com/about-us/ things-
  thatmatter-to-us.html>.

Hyatt Hotels and Resorts. N.p., n.d. Web. 9 May 2012.
  <http://www.hyatt.com/hyatt/index.jsp>.

IBM. N.p., n.d. Web. 9 May 2012.
  <http://www.ibm. com/us/en/>.

IKEA. N.p., n.d. Web 23 Feb 2023. <Vision, culture and
  values - IKEA (jobs.cz)>.

Kaiser, Marian Shalander, and Michael Mitilier. *Rule of
  Thumb: A Guide to Small Business Basics*. Omaha:
  Write Life, 2010. Print.

Kraft Foods. N.p., n.d. Web. 8 May 2012. <http://www.
  kraftfoodscompany.com/welcome.aspx>.

Linnell, Deborah, Zora Radosevich, and Jonathon
  Spack. *Executive Directors Guide: The Guide For
  Successful Nonprofit Management*. Boston: United
  Way of Massachusetts Bay, 2002. Print.

Lowes. N.p., n.d. Web. 28 Feb. 2023. <Our Strategy |
  Lowe's Corporate (lowes.com)>.

McDonald's. N.p., n.d. Web. 9 May 2012.
 <http://www. mcdonalds.com/us/ en/home.html>.

Metropolitan Community College. N.p., n.d. Web. 8 May
  2012. <http://www.mccneb.edu/>.

Nike. Nike Mission Statement 2022 | Nike Mission &
Vision Analysis (mission-statement.com)

Omaha Public Schools. N.p., n.d. Web. 8 May 2012.
<http://www.ops.org/ district/ CENTRALOFFICES/
OfficeoftheSuperintendent/MissionStatement/tabid/
199/Default.aspx>.

Oregon Shakespeare Festival. N.p., n.d. Web. 8 May 2012.
<http://www.osfashland.org/>.

Quigley, Joseph V. *Vision: How Leaders Develop It, Share
It, and Sustain It*. New York: McGraw, 1993. Print.

Romero, Jose Luis. "Sample Vision Statements."
Skills2Lead.com. SiteSell.com, n.d. Web. 19
Mar. 2012.

Sony Corporation. N.p., n.d. Web. 27 Feb. 2023.
<https://mission-statement.com/sony/>.

Southwest Airlines. N.p., n.d. Web. 27 Feb. 2023.
<Purpose, Vision, and The Southwest Way –
Southwest Airlines
(southwestairlinesinvestorrelations.com)>.

Starbucks. N.p., n.d. Web. 27 Feb. 2023.
<https://parnmore.com/starbucks-coffee-vision-
statement-mission-statement.com>.

Teach for America. N.p., n.d. Web. 28 Feb. 2023.
<https://www.teachforamerica.org/what-we-
do/our-values>.

TED. N.p., n.d. Web 27 Feb. 2023. <Our mission: Spread
ideas, foster community and create impact | About
| TED>.

Warby Parker. N.p. n.d. Web. 27 Feb. 2023. <Warby
Parker Mission Statement 2023 | Warby Parker

Mission & Vision Analysis (mission-statement.com)>

Whole Foods Market. N.p., n.d. Web. 27 Feb. 2023. <http://mission-statement.com/whole-foods-market/>.

Zappos. N.p., n.d. Web. 9 May 2012. <http://www.zappos.com/?gclid=CLrkxq_3868CFaJgTAodrjDL Zg>.

Author Biography

Sonia Keffer is the owner of Keffer and Associates, a consulting and training company focused on helping entrepreneurs and small business build on their ideas to generate action. improving leadership skills and team cohesion. Sonia has been consulting with both non-profit and for-profit companies on leadership and team development issues for over twenty-five years. A main focus of Sonia's work is the internal motivation that is necessary for all of us to be truly successful. Keffer enjoys bringing new ideas to all levels of employees and seeing the spark ignite in people when they understand how to incorporate a new concept into their lives. Sonia has been fortunate enough to work across the United States with such organizations as Curtis and Associates, Inc.; the County of Orange, CA; California, the City and County of San Francisco, CA. In her hometown of Omaha, Nebraska, Sonia has worked with such terrific organizations as Fashion Cleaners, Concord Mediation Center, Omaha Public Schools, Gavilon, Valmont, PVPL, the Nebraska Arts Council, the Nebraska Shakespeare Festival, the University of Nebraska at Omaha, the Nonprofit Association of the Midlands, and the Small Business Association of the Midlands, as well as, Metropolitan Community College, the AIM Institute, and Creighton University.

To learn more about Sonia's work, visit her website, www.soniakeffer.com.